BIRDS

An Illustrated Treasury

Compiled by Michelle Lovric

COURAGE BOOKS

an imprint of
RUNNING PRESS
Philadelphia, Pennsylvania

Library of Congress Cataloging-in-Publication Number 92–50182
ISBN 1–56138–173–X
Text edited by Melissa Stein
Cover design by Toby Schmidt
Cover illustration by Raymond Watson
Typography by Commcor Communications Corporation, Philadelphia, Pennsylvania

Published by Courage Books, an imprint of Running Press Book Publishers
125 South Twenty-second Street
Philadelphia, Pennsylvania 19103

The author gratefully acknowledges the permission of the following to reproduce copyrighted material in this book:

p. 6: From *Green Thoughts: A Writer in the Garden* by Eleanor Perényi, published by Random House Inc., New York, and Allen Lane, London. Copyright © Eleanor Perényi, 1981.

p. 18: From *Captive Bird* by Boethius, translated by Helen Waddell, from *More Latin Lyrics*, edited by Dame Felicitas Corrigan, published by Victor Gollanez Ltd., London. Copyright © Stanbrook Abbey 1976.

THREE OF THE MOST INTRIGUING CONCEPTS KNOWN TO US—BEAUTY, MUSIC, AND FLIGHT—FIND THEIR ELOQUENT UNION IN BIRDS. *Introduction*

BIRDS PERSONIFY THE CHANGING SEASONS BOTH IN NATURE AND IN HUMAN LIFE, SIGNALING BY THEIR MIGRATION THE BEGINNING OR END OF A CYCLE. IN THE LIVES OF BIRDS WE FIND MANY DISTINCTIVE PARALLELS TO OUR OWN: BIRDS CHERISH FREEDOM AS WELL AS CLOSE FAMILY LIFE; THEY NOURISH AND EDUCATE THEIR YOUNG WITH TENDERNESS; THEY EAGERLY COMMUNICATE WITH EACH OTHER IN A COMPLEX LANGUAGE. THE FRENCH ANTHROPOLOGIST CLAUDE LEVI-STRAUSS OBSERVED THAT WHAT MOST SEPARATES BIRDS FROM HUMANS IS THE BOUNDLESS ELEMENT IN WHICH THEY ARE PRIVILEGED TO MOVE.

THE BIRD WORLD CAN SEEM A METAPHOR FOR HUMAN SOCIETY, AND HAS INSPIRED A WEALTH OF FINE LITERATURE. WITH THEIR EXQUISITE FORMS AND VIVID COLORS, BIRDS ALSO HAVE INSPIRED WORKS OF EXTRAORDINARY ARTISTIC SENSITIVITY. THE IMAGES HERE HAVE BEEN CHOSEN IN CELEBRATION OF THESE SPIRITED SOARERS.

Prettie Redbreast, Sing,

What I would speake.

GEORGE DANIEL (1616–1657)
ENGLISH POET

. . . SOME THINGS—BIRDS LIKE WALKING FABLES—OUGHT TO INHABIT NOWHERE

BUT THE REVERENCE OF THE HEART.

Judith Wright, b. 1915
Australian poet and critic

I cherish the mourning doves, the cardinals whistling farewell to the day, and the rare visitations of evening grosbeaks and bluebirds that make one feel, quite unjustifiably, like one of the chosen.

ELEANOR PERÉNYI
20TH-CENTURY AMERICAN WRITER

I ONCE HAD A SPARROW ALIGHT ON MY

SHOULDER FOR A MOMENT WHILE I WAS

HOEING IN A VILLAGE GARDEN, AND I

FELT THAT I WAS MORE DISTINGUISHED

BY THAT CIRCUMSTANCE THAN I SHOULD

HAVE BEEN BY ANY EPAULET I COULD

HAVE WORN.

Henry David Thoreau (1817–1862)
American writer

That's the wise thrush; he sings each song twice over,

Lest you should think he never could recapture

That first fine careless rapture!

ROBERT BROWNING (1812–1889)
ENGLISH POET

[The blackbird]...sings in a quiet, leisurely way, as a great artist should.

RICHARD JEFFERIES (1848–1887)
ENGLISH NATURALIST

Lark-like

sings the

soaring soul.

GEORGE MEREDITH (1828–1909)
ENGLISH NOVELIST AND POET

. . . TO LISTEN TO STARS AND BIRDS, TO BABES AND SAGES, WITH OPEN HEART . . . .

THIS IS TO BE MY SYMPHONY.

William Henry Channing (1810–1884)
American cleric

We never miss the music till the sweet-voiced bird has flown.

O. Henry [William Sydney Porter] (1862–1910)
American writer

Thou wast not born for death, immortal Bird!
No hungry generations tread thee down;
The voice I hear this passing night was heard
In ancient days . . .

John Keats (1795–1821)
English poet

fourteen

Ask me no more whither doth haste

The nightingale, when May is past;

For in your sweet dividing throat

She winters, and keeps warm her note.

THOMAS CAREW (1598–1639)
ENGLISH POET

EVEN WHEN THE BIRD WALKS ONE FEELS THAT IT HAS WINGS.

Antoine-Marin Lemierre (1733–1793)
French writer

*The reason birds can fly
and we can't is simply
that they have perfect faith,
for faith is to have wings.*

J. M. BARRIE (1860–1937)
SCOTTISH WRITER

THE JOY OF LIFE . . . IS VERY GREAT . . . THE SOFT LOVING COO OF THE DOVE IN THE

HAWTHORNE; THE BLACKBIRD RUFFLING OUT HIS FEATHERS ON A RAIL. THE SENSE

OF LIVING—THE CONSCIOUSNESS OF SEEING AND FEELING—IS MANIFESTLY INTENSE

IN THEM ALL, AND IS IN ITSELF AN EXQUISITE PLEASURE.

Richard Jefferies (1848–1887)
English naturalist

The bird was happy once in the high trees,

You cage it in your cellar, bring it seed,

Honey to sip, all that its heart can need

Or human love can think of: till it sees,

Leaping too high within its narrow room

The old familiar shadow of the leaves,

And spurns the seed with tiny desperate claws.

Naught but the woods despairing pleads,

The woods, the woods again, it grieves, it grieves.

ANICIUS MANLIUS SEVERINUS BOETHIUS (480–524)
ROMAN STATESMAN AND PHILOSOPHER

...LIKE A SUMMER BIRD-CAGE IN A GARDEN, THE BIRDS THAT ARE WITHOUT DESPAIR TO GET IN, AND BIRDS THAT ARE WITHIN DESPAIR AND ARE IN A CONSUMPTION FOR FEAR THEY SHALL NEVER GET OUT.

John Webster (1580–1625)
English dramatist

No bird soars too high, if he soars with his own wings.

WILLIAM BLAKE (1757–1827)
ENGLISH WRITER AND ARTIST

THE WILD DUCKS WESTWARD FLY,

AND MAKE ABOVE MY ANXIOUS HEAD

TRIANGLES IN THE SKY.

Indian poem, translated by Laurence Hope
[Adela Florence Nicholson] (1812–1883)
English writer

WHATEVER SPECIAL NESTS WE MAKE—

LEAVES AND MOSS LIKE THE MARMOTS

AND BIRDS, OR TENTS AND PILED STONE

—WE ALL DWELL IN A HOUSE OF ONE

ROOM—THE WORLD WITH THE FIRMA-

MENT FOR ITS ROOF—AND ARE SAILING

THE CELESTIAL SPACES WITHOUT LEAV-

ING ANY TRACK.

John Muir (1838–1914)
Scottish-born American naturalist

. . . honoring heaven, the bird
traverses
the transparency, without soiling
the day.

PABLO NERUDA (1904–1973)
CHILEAN POET AND DIPLOMAT

Hail to thee, blithe Spirit!

Bird thou never wert,

That from heaven, or near it,

Pourest thy full heart

In profuse strains of unpremeditated art.

PERCY BYSSHE SHELLEY (1792–1822)
ENGLISH POET

ALONE AND WARMING HIS FIVE WITS,
THE WHITE OWL IN THE BELFRY SITS.

Alfred, Lord Tennyson (1809–1892)
English poet

In order to see birds it is necessary to become a part of the silence.

ROBERT LYND (1879–1949)
IRISH JOURNALIST

The moping owl does to the moon complain. . .

THOMAS GRAY (1716–1771)
ENGLISH POET

𝒲hate'er birds did or dreamed,
[the mockingbird] could say.

SYDNEY LANIER (1842–1881)
AMERICAN POET

DO YOU NE'ER THINK WHAT WONDROUS BEINGS THESE?

DO YOU NE'ER THINK WHO MADE THEM, AND WHO TAUGHT

THE DIALECT THEY SPEAK, WHERE MELODIES

ALONE ARE THE INTERPRETERS OF THOUGHT?

Henry Wadsworth Longfellow (1807–1882)
American writer

Keep a green tree in your heart and perhaps a singing bird will come.

CHINESE PROVERB

O NE

SWALLOW DOES NOT

MAKE A SUMMER.

Aristotle (384–322 B.C.)
Greek philosopher

One swallow does not make a summer,

but one skein of geese, cleaving the

murk of a March thaw, is the Spring.

ALDO LEOPOLD (1886–1948)
AMERICAN WRITER AND CONSERVATIONIST

WHEN ROBIN'S NOT A BEGGAR,

AND JENNY WREN'S A BRIDE,

AND LARKS HANG SINGING,

SINGING, SINGING

OVER THE WHEAT-FIELDS WIDE . . .

Christina Rossetti (1830–1894)
English poet

Solitary the thrush,

The hermit withdrawn to himself,

    avoiding the settlements,

Sings by himself a song.

WALT WHITMAN (1819–1892)
AMERICAN POET

...thrush

Through echoing timber does so rinse and wring

The ear, it strikes like lightning to hear him sing.

GERARD MANLEY HOPKINS (1844–1899)
ENGLISH POET

THE LITTLE NIGHTINGALE . . . HAD

COME TO SING OF COMFORT AND HOPE.

AS HE SANG . . . THE BLOOD FLOWED

QUICKER AND QUICKER THROUGH THE

EMPEROR'S FEEBLE BODY. EVEN DEATH

LISTENED AND SAID, "GO ON, LITTLE

NIGHTINGALE, GO ON!"

Hans Christian Andersen (1805–1875)
Danish writer

THE SONGS OF THE BIRDS WERE SO PLEASANT THAT IT SEEMED A MAN COULD NEVER WISH TO LEAVE THE PLACE. THE FLOCKS OF PARROTS CONCEALED THE SUN; AND THE BIRDS WERE SO NUMEROUS, AND OF SO MANY DIFFERENT KINDS, THAT IT WAS WONDERFUL.

Christopher Columbus (1451–1506)
Spanish explorer

It is very pretty to see the House Martins . . . collecting mud for their nests. Their short feathered legs look quite as if they had little white socks on.

EDITH HOLDEN (1871–1920)
ENGLISH NATURALIST

How do you know

but ev'ry Bird that cuts the airy way,

Is an immense world of delight,

clos'd by your senses five?

WILLIAM BLAKE (1757–1827)
ENGLISH WRITER AND ARTIST

Magic birds were dancing in the mystic marsh. The grass swayed with them, and the shallow waters, and the earth fluttered under them. The earth was dancing with the cranes, and the low sun, and the wind and sky.

Marjorie Kinnan Rawlings (1896–1953)
American writer

It is not only fine feathers that
make fine birds.

AESOP
SIXTH-CENTURY B.C. GREEK WRITER

BEING BORN IN A DUCK YARD DOES NOT MATTER, IF ONLY YOU ARE HATCHED FROM A SWAN'S EGG.

Hans Christian Andersen (1805–1875)
Danish writer

It is astonishing how violently a big branch shakes when a silly little bird has left it. I expect the bird knows it and feels immensely arrogant.

KATHERINE MANSFIELD (1888–1924)
ENGLISH WRITER

He clasps the crag with crooked hands;

Close to the sun in lonely lands,

Ringed with the azure world, he stands.

The wrinkled sea beneath him crawls;

He watches from his mountain walls,

And like a thunderbolt he falls.

ALFRED, LORD TENNYSON (1809–1892)
ENGLISH POET

YOU MUST NOT KNOW TOO MUCH, OR BE TOO PRECISE OR SCIENTIFIC ABOUT

BIRDS AND TREES AND FLOWERS . . . A CERTAIN FREE MARGIN, AND EVEN VAGUENESS,

PERHAPS IGNORANCE, CREDULITY—HELPS YOUR ENJOYMENT OF THESE THINGS.

Walt Whitman (1819–1892)
American poet

SAW A KINGFISHER SKIMMING ACROSS A

POND BY THE ROADSIDE, IT MADE A

GLOWING PICTURE, WITH ITS EMERALD

PLUMAGE AGAINST THE DARK BROWN

WATER AND THE OVERHANGING BOUGHS

OF A MAPLE TREE ALL GOLD AND RED . . .

Edith Holden (1871–1920)
English naturalist

Birds are, perhaps, the most eloquent expression of reality.

ROGER TORY PETERSON, B. 1908
AMERICAN ORNITHOLOGIST

ILLUSTRATION ACKNOWLEDGMENTS

COVER: *House Sparrows*, Raymond Watson

p.1 [detail]: *Goldcrests*, Chris Shields

p.4: *Robin*, Basil Ede

p.6,7 [detail]: *Turtle Dove*, Chris Shields

p.9: *Wrens in Plant Pot*, Peter Swan-Brown

p.10 [detail]: *Goldcrests*, Chris Shields

p.12: *Dotterel and Sundew*, Archibald Thorburn

p.14: *The New Brood*, Edward Neale (Fine Art Photographic Library Limited)

p.16: *Dipper*, Basil Ede

p.19: *Grey Heron*, Chris Shields

p.21: *Lapwing*, Archibald Thorburn

p.22: *Wrens*, Chris Shields

p.24, 25 [detail]: *Blue Tit*, Basil Ede

p.26: *Little Owl*, Basil Ede

p.29 [detail]: *Waxwing*, Chris Shields

p.31: *Swallow and Lamp*, David Blackmore

p.32, 33 [detail]: *Nuthatch*, Chris Shields

p.34,35 [detail]: *Greenfinch*, Basil Ede

p.37: *House Martins*, Archibald Thorburn

p.39: *Cuckoo and Wren*, David Blackmore

p.41: *Long-Tailed Titmouse with Rose Hips*, Basil Ede

p.42 [detail]: *Goldfinches*, Basil Ede

p.45: *Great Tit*, Chris Shields